RUSH

BRIAN HARRIGAN

Omnibus Press

London/New York/Sydney/Cologne

Published 1982 by Omnibus Press
(A division of Book Sales Limited)

Art director: Mike Bell
Book designed by: Delaney & Ireland
Picture research by: Valerie Boyd
Picture credits:
Paul Canty/LFI 13, 35 *top*, 38 *top left*, 60/61
Fin Costello Cover, 3, 5, 12, 16, 17, 20 *top*, 24, 25, 27, 28, 30/31, 33, 34 *bottom left*, 35 *bottom*, 36/37, 38 *top right*, 38 *bottom*, 40/41, 42 *top right*, 42 *bottom*, 43 *top*, 44, 45, 46 *top*, 46 *bottom*, 47, 48, 51, 53, 54/55, 55 *inset*, 57, 58/59, 60 *left*, 62, 63, 66/67, 68, 70, 71, 72, 76, 77, 78, 79, 80
Fin Costello/LFI 39 *top*, 44 *bottom*
Paul Cox/LFI 18/19, 20*bottom*, 22, 23, 39 *centre*, 39 *bottom*, 42 *top left*, 65, 74/75
Simon Fowler/LFI 34 *top*, 57 *inset*
Gary Gershof/LFI 9
Mercury 7, 10/11, 14

Exclusive distributors:

Book Sales Limited
78 Newman Street, London W1P 3LA
England

The Putnam Publishing Group
200 Madison Avenue, New York,
N.Y.10016 USA

Omnibus Press
139 King Street, Sydney, NSW 2000
Australia

Music Sales GmbH
Kolner Strasse 199, D-5000 Cologne
90 West Germany

To The Music Trade Only:

Music Sales Limited
78 Newman Street, London W1P 3LA
England

Music Sales Corporation
799 Broadway, New York, N.Y.10003
USA

ISBN 0.86001.934.9
OP 41292

Typeset by Futurafoto Ltd
Printed in England by:
Wm. Clowes (Beccles) Limited,
London & Beccles

PLYMOUTH
MICH
WELLCOME'S
TOURING NORTH

RUSH

The first time I saw Rush – the first time I actually met them – was Sunday, February 12, 1978. That was the opening date of their second British tour. They were set to do 16 dates in all, kicking off at Birmingham Odeon.

At the time I was a press officer with Phonogram Records, who released Rush's records in this country on the Mercury label.

I travelled to Birmingham with two other Phonogram employees – artist liaison man John Burnham and product manager Alan Phillips. On the way we speculated on how well the band would do. Their 'Farewell To Kings' album had been released at the end of the previous year and had been selling well. In addition they had a staunch supporter in the shape of Geoff Barton who had given the band immense exposure in *Sounds*. On the other hand, though, the boom in hard rock, heavy metal, symphonic rock, pomp-rock – call it what you will – had not yet developed to the extent it would in 1979 and 1980.

The sort of places Rush were booked to play were concert halls of three and a half to four thousand capacity. I remember suggesting that maybe the band had bitten off a little more than they could chew.

We arrived at Birmingham a little later than we needed to, had a quick plate full of grease, eggs, and bacon at a local greasy spoon and wandered next door to the Odeon.

By the time we had wandered into the auditorium the band were just coming on stage. They were greeted with an ear-wobbling roar. The audience rose to its feet and I looked around to find that the place was packed tighter than a squat for sardines. I was amazed, but this response didn't prepare me for the show that followed. It still ranks in my all-time top five of live gigs. The sound was immaculate, the lighting superb, the music perfection and the performance superb.

We rushed backstage to see them afterwards – the band, the road crew, their managers, and there I met Geddy Lee, Alex Lifeson and Neil Peart for the first time. To my surprise they weren't all seven foot tall, nor were they exhibiting any signs of halos or celestial glows. There were just three quiet men sitting in their dressing room chatting to each other.

We suggested a party to celebrate this most spectacular and successful opening night of a tour. They looked at each other and then suggested that maybe they would prefer just to go back to their hotel, order tea and ice cream from room service and crash out early.

I couldn't believe it. Being on the road with a rock band is supposed to be synonymous with getting smashed and generally behaving in a manner that would get the average person chucked out of one of the more extreme night spots in Hamburg.

An unusual band, I mused to myself back at the hotel as Burnham and I had a playful game of darts using a particularly abysmal painting in the room as a board. I decided I'd have to see more of them.

On that tour I went on to see them in Newcastle, Glasgow, London (two nights), Sheffield, Manchester and Southampton. Each night was a revelation. The show was as precisely perfect, and yet still remarkably fresh, at every concert. In addition, every night was a sell-out. It eventually dawned on even my feeble brain that I was witnessing a rock and roll phenomenon. I was seeing a band break through to the major league in Britain on only their second tour of the country.

It shouldn't have taken me to the end of the tour in Southampton to realise this, of course. If I'd done my homework a bit earlier I would have seen long before the tour began that Rush were a huge band. That British tour was a sell-out two solid months before it started. Their first half dozen albums were selling as fast as they could be brought into the country to a hardcore but rapidly burgeoning legion of fans. What they were doing was breaking through in Britain in exactly the same inevitable, inexorable manner that they had done in their native Canada and neighbouring United States.

What more can I say? I, like hundreds of thousands of others had become a believer. But then Rush aren't a bad choice of a band to believe in.

Geddy Lee and Alex Lifeson met in Sarnia, a suburb of Toronto. Alex was born in Fernie, British Columbia, and Geddy came from Willowdale. When they were 15 years old and still in high school, they teamed up with a friend of Lifeson's called John Rutsey in order to play some of the music that they enjoyed listening to.

Their influences were Led Zeppelin, Cream, Jimi Hendrix, Grand Funk Railroad and Iron Butterfly and at first they were merely a group of friends rehearsing inconspicuously together and occasionally branching out to do the odd local high school dance or private party.

They drifted into the bar and club circuit when, at the beginning of the 1970s the Canadian province of Ontario reduced its legal drinking age from 21 to 18 – thus allowing the band to legally enter such premises.

Despite being a hard working band – insofar as they could get gigs, which wasn't easy at the time – there was little to distinguish them from any other bunch of small-time musicians. That is, if you don't count the prodigious volume they played at, according to legend.

Perhaps one of the most fortunate things in the band's early career was that they came into contact with a gentleman by the name of Ray Danniels who first met them when he promoted a show for them at a South Ontario school. He was 16 years old at the time. He later became their manager, selling his own management agency to help raise money to record Rush's first album and teaming up with Vic Wilson who was also an agent.

STRATOCASTER

Towards the end of 1973 Wilson and Danniels fixed Rush up with a support gig for The New York Dolls at a concert hall in Toronto. It was the biggest audience they had faced in their four year career. Geddy Lee later said that their performance on that night wasn't particularly impressive from the band's point of view simply because the audience was so big.

However, due to their immense amount of rehearsing and live gigging together, Rush put on a competent show which easily outshone The Dolls who had never, in their career, really raised themselves above a sort of studied, decadent musical shambles.

It was at this point that Rush realised they could hold their own in big halls in front of large audiences and they made a conscious decision, with Wilson and Danniels, to go after bigger and better shows – despite the fact that they would almost certainly lose money which they could scarcely afford.

Danniels and Wilson, in the meantime, managed to raise the cash to buy the band some studio time. They realised that an album had to be released as soon as possible if the band was not to lose its momentum. By recording late at night and in small chunks at a time they managed to buy studio time at a low rate. In addition, they saved more money by getting a local, unknown producer to take care of the finished sound for them.

That was the point where their career damn near stopped in its tracks. The finished album was far short of what they had expected. It was flat and lifeless and both the band and their managers realised that it wouldn't get them anywhere in the sales market.

They raised more money and got hold of another local producer but one who at least had a track record having worked with Canadian outfits April Wine and Thundermug plus Britain's Procol Harum. That man's name was Terry Brown who, as any Rush fan

knows, was to figure large in their career. He and the band entered Toronto Sound Studios and in $9000 worth of studio time Brown did a hero's job, capturing the original roughness and raucous power which the band knew they had put down on tape. The next step was to find a label that would release the album.

Nothing doing. No-one was interested, though Danniels and Wilson demonstrated their willingness to do any sort of deal at all just to get the album into the market place and stand a chance of selling.

So they decided to set up their own label and release it themselves. It says much for the tenacity and self-belief that Rush and Wilson and Danniels had that such a step would seem logical. The new label was called Moon Records and put out the first Rush album, simply titled 'Rush', in a limited fashion in Ontario. With little or no money available to them Rush couldn't afford the sort of promotional and advertising activity that one normally associates with the release of a rock album. They were just hoping that their live work and the honourable tradition of word of mouth would do the trick for them. It did. The initial pressings of the album sold out rapidly and created something of a stir.

Copies of the 'Rush' album were imported into the United States and one of them ended up in the hands of the musical director of Cleveland, Ohio, radio station WMMS, Donna Halper. She was so impressed that she drew the attention of Mercury Records and New York booking agency ATI to the existence of this hot new Canadian outfit that didn't even have a record deal in the States. Halper reported to Mercury, ATI and the band themselves (a friend of whom had sent the record to Halper) that on the strength of just playing one track on the radio the station had received at least 50 telephone calls from listeners wanting to know who the band was and where they could get a copy of the album.

Both ATI and Mercury signed the band up. In the case of the latter it's probable that two external factors helped Rush to break through this most important of barriers – being picked up by a major record company.

The first was that Mercury had The New York Dolls contracted to them and there seems little doubt that reports of Rush's successful Toronto gig with The Dolls had filtered back to the company. Secondly, Mercury also had Bachman Turner Overdrive on their books – a Canadian band who Mercury prided themselves on having discovered and who were making the company a lot of money through international record sales. It seemed, no doubt, providential to Mercury that another band from Canada should also be falling into their laps.

All credit to Mercury though. They contracted Rush to a two album deal and shelled out 200,000 dollars for the privilege – no mean example of confidence, considering that no Canadian record company seemed to fancy Rush at any price.

Between the release of 'Rush' in July, 1974 and the end of the year the album sold around 75,000 copies in the United States alone. However, round about this time, just as Rush could have been forgiven for thinking they'd finally cracked it, they were faced with a major problem. John Rutsey quit the band citing health reasons. He also had different ideas from Lee and Lifeson about the musical direction the band should take.

Geddy Lee recalled later that Rutsey's health really was bad as a result, he reckoned, of the gruelling live schedule that the band had set itself right from its beginning.

The departure of Rutsey was a major crisis point for Rush. The ATI agency had fixed them up with an extensive series of dates in the United States and now Rush didn't have a drummer.

With the tour coming up in August, 1974, – remember, their all-important début jaunt outside of their native Canada – Rush had to find a replacement. They did – a gentleman by the name of Neil Peart.

Peart was to have a radical effect on Rush's future. As a drummer he has been rated among the best rockers in the world but more important to the development of the band was his remarkable skill as a lyricist.

Growing up near Toronto Peart had been a voracious reader, immersing himself in science fiction of all kinds, C.S. Lewis, J.R.R. Tolkien and Russian-born authoress the late Ayn Rand (remember that last name – it gets really important later on). These days he still tends to read everything he can lay his hands on from Plato to Agatha Christie to Thomas Hardy and still more science fiction and fantasy.

He was interested in music from an early age. His parents sent him to piano lessons but he didn't particularly take to them, instead he expressed a greater interest in the more rhythmic side of music. So they gave in to the inevitable and paid for a year and a half of drum lessons from the time he was 13 years old.

In the beginning Peart was most interested in the late Keith Moon of The Who and his aggressive style of drumming. Later he began to pick up on Carl Palmer, Bill Bruford, Michael Giles (the first drummer with King Crimson) and so on – the more technically orientated percussionists.

Like Lee and Lifeson, Peart went to high school where he began to get involved in playing in school bands. He played with small-time outfits around his home area and then, at the beginning of the Seventies, went to London to see if it was possible to make a full-time living out of music in what was then the rock capital of the world.

Unlike fellow Canadian Pat Travers who was later to do precisely that, Peart had no luck. He ended up selling souvenirs in London's tourist trap, Carnaby Street, before returning home when the money and the impetus ran out.

He took a job as a salesman with his father who dealt in farm equipment and eventually ended up as parts manager. At the same time, though, Peart still maintained his connections with the music business.

Anyway, with time running out for the start of Rush's first tour of the States and the band still not having a drummer, Danniels and Wilson were desperately looking for a replacement for the departed John Rutsey. After auditioning several who weren't up to scratch Rush remembered Peart as being a drummer in the area who had sounded interesting The managers got in touch with Peart, he auditioned and got the gig. Says

Peart: "It just seemed to work out perfectly. We seemed to be musically suited to each other and I seemed to fit in with the kind of future directions they were talking about. Besides that we fitted together well personally – we found we had a lot of things in common." Quite how much impact Peart was to make on the band didn't manifest itself until the fourth album, '2112', was released in March, 1976. But that's getting ahead of the story.

Rush's first tour of the States lasted from August 19, 1974, to December 20 with the trio playing dates with bands like Rory Gallagher, Uriah Heep, Blue Oyster Cult, the Italian pomp-rock band PFM, Rare Earth, Manfred Mann and Wet Willie.

The critics saw the band in wildly different lights. *Cashbox*, reporting from a gig in New Jersey in October of 1974 was unaware that John Rutsey was no longer in the band and suggested that he (Rutsey) was "a driving musician." Geddy was likened, not for the first time in his life, to Robert Plant, and overall Rush were considered "a hard driving rocking and rolling band very reminiscent of some early Led Zeppelin."

Billboard quietly enthused about the same gig rating Geddy as a vocalist of exceptional range, suggesting that Alex Lifeson displayed stimulating guitar showmanship and that "there are no frills to the band's music and it offers nothing new or startling, just a straightforward approach that is used to best effect on their original compositions."

For Al Rudis in the *Chicago Sun-Times* Rush were nothing more than "a Canadian group that appeared to be moving into the void left by Grand Funk Railroad and Black Sabbath."

Pride of place, however, might well be saved for a gentleman by the name of Marc Shapiro who, writing for the *Hollywood Daily News* about a date at the Whisky A Go Go, said: "Rush's gig at the Whisky last night can best be described as heavy metal tedium. The Canadian entry into the 'let's learn three chords and become the new Black Sabbath' derby relied on cliché riffs throughout its set and only twice did this reporter perceive of anything resembling an imaginative riff."

He concluded by suggesting a couple of Rush's numbers were "predictable in the classic power trio mould and point to definite possibilities for the band on the less discriminating cheap wine and reds circuit."

The "reds" reference, by the way, is about downers, or barbiturates, which is quite a popular cliché when writers are talking about loud and heavy bands which they don't particularly like as in "The only way to listen to Black Sabbath is with a bottle of red wine in one hand and a fistful of reds in the other."

For the most part, however, reviews tended to be quite favourable, if not exactly overwhelmingly enthusiastic, and Rush could have been forgiven for thinking that they were off to a reasonable start in the States.

After a short break over Christmas Rush were back in Toronto Sound studios to record their second album, 'Fly By Night'. It was January 1975.

Oddly enough this follow-up album had a lot to live up to. I say oddly enough because from the perspective of the Eighties 'Rush' is very much the odd record out in the Rush collection. It's a gutsy hard rocker, lacking the symphonic, lyrical content, the intelligence and literary style of subsequent collections.

However, 'Rush', was the biggest selling début album that Mercury had enjoyed in the States, even outshining fellow Canadians Bachman Turner Overdrive's first. And all this despite the fact that the first attempt at 'Rush' had been done in Toronto's Eastern Studios in just eight hours after a gig, and that the clean up operation with Terry Brown re-mixing and re-producing was done in just three days. It also might be added that John Rutsey had been considered the band's chief lyricist and when he declared his intention of dropping out from the band Geddy Lee had had to fill the gap – a task which he hadn't relished.

Peart, however, slid neatly into his new and additional role of lyric writer, at the same time lending an inspirational touch to Lifeson and Lee. 'Fly By Night' boasted such gems as 'By-Tor And The Snow Dog,' a classic tale of good versus evil couched in mythological personalities, 'Rivendell' inspired by the village of the same name in J.R.R. Tolkien's Lord Of The Rings, and of course 'Anthem'.

The latter was inspired by the novel of the same name by the aforementioned Ayn Rand, an authoress who first became established in the Thirties and one who had been read extensively by Peart.

"Anthem", published in 1938 remains Rand's best known book. Rand, born in Petrograd, Russia – later to become Leningrad after the Russian revolution – emigrated to the United States where she carved out a career as a playwright, novelist and film writer. Her pronounced right-wing views were presumably a counterblast to what she had seen happen to her native Russia.

Her novel "Anthem" is set in a totalitarian state sited in a closed city. The rulers of this particular society have declared that personality should be non-existent, there should be no individuality and no rights. This anti-personality credo even extends as far as the outlawing of the word "I". However, two rebels rediscover individuality and break away.

Peart himself is very much a believer in individuality. He's stated repeatedly in the past that he can't believe in a completely egalitarian society because it's patently obvious that people are not equal. It's this sturdy and unbending faith in his own ideas, as unfashionable as they may be that has landed Peart in the centre of controversy more than once. But he remains defiant and unrepentant. He once told me heatedly: "I'm not a Fascist. I'm not some extremist. Yes, I'm a capitalist and I believe in self-reliance – but not without caring for other people. Actually I'm tired of talking about this. You say what you like about the whole thing. You know enough about the band to get it right."

In that particular case Peart was talking about a much later event – a notable destruction job done by Miles in the *NME* in 1977, centred round 'Anthem' and the later album, very much an expanded version of the same theme, '2112'.

Back to 1975, however. 'Fly By Night' was released in North America in February 1975 at the same time as Rush received their first major award.

That was the Juno Award – Canada's equivalent to the American Grammy – as the nation's most promising new group. Says Geddy Lee: "That was a great help to us in Canada. It brought us a lot of attention from a lot of people who hadn't heard of us or people who didn't really take us seriously. But it didn't really help us much anywhere else."

Quite so. Despite the enormous amount of talent that has emerged from Canada, the United States, its southern neighbour, has remained steadfastly unimpressed by the nation's musical credibility. Being big in Canada, as far as the States is concerned, means about as much as being big in Belgium does in Britain.

However, Rush have never been a band to be daunted just by being ignored.

Managers Danniels and Wilson and the band have always been subscribers to the theory that to gain a following among fans you have to get out on the road. That's what Rush have done for most of their career.

"We used to do about 200 concerts a year", says Lifeson "taking about nine months followed by maybe a couple of months in the recording studio."

So, with their Juno Award safely in the bag and 'Fly By Night' out on the streets Rush set off on their second tour of the States, a four month long stint supporting Aerosmith and Kiss.

Needless to say Rush still weren't exactly loaded financially and for transport on much of the tour they had to hire a car. Alex Lifeson later told Rolling Stone magazine that they told the car hire firm in Toronto they were just going to use the vehicle for a few dates. They brought it back with 11,000 miles on the clock, no hubcaps, a broken radio and no mirror. "It was ruined", he said mildly. "They were quite surprised."

This was a better tour than the previous one for Rush. First they were linked with bands who would bring in far larger numbers of people than on their previous, ground-breaking jaunt round the States. And secondly they had material to play which was much more suited to the three piece line-up of Lifeson, Peart and Lee.

They returned to Toronto in July to begin work on their third album, 'Caress Of Steel' which picked up where 'Fly By Night' had left off.

Previously, by the way, the band had fulfilled an ambition by doing their own headlining tour of Canada which included a sell-out performance at Toronto's 4,000 seater Massey Hall which for all of them was the realisation of an ambition. "We'd never been able to do a tour of Canada or even the midwest of the country before," said Lifeson. "Everyone said heavy metal was dead and gone and we were out of fashion." Peart added that to play Massey Hall was one of his first great ambitions and he used to dream of being on the stage there.

'Caress' was released in North America in September 1975 and it proved a further step up in the band's career – both commercially and musically.

The album featured the exquisitely melodic 'Lakeside Park', the amusing 'I Think I'm Going Bald' and a welcome return of By-Tor who meets up with the 'Necromancer'. Best of all, though, one whole side of the record was devoted to 'Fountain Of Lamneth' a typically allegorical, mythological, lyrical and almost hermetic piece of writing by Peart.

In all it was an epic effort and the final stamp of authenticity on Rush's claim to be more than just a head-bashing band in the tradition of Grand Funk and Blue Cheer.

With that ambition realised, they were off on tour round the continent of North America again. This was another near four month long trek which saw Rush achieving the status of special guests in some areas and as headliners – for the first time in the States – in others. At the same time the band began to notice that their music was being heard internationally.

Import sales of their first three albums began to show significant increases in countries such as Germany, Sweden and Holland, while Japan reported the presence of a Rush fan club. By March of 1976 'Fly By Night' had been certified a gold album in Canada, while 'Caress Of Steel' had racked up around 40,000 sales in Canada alone.

However, as pleasant as that might have been, Rush's minds were elsewhere. They were concentrating on completing their fourth album – '2112'.

Soon after the release of '2112' Geddy Lee explained in interview after interview that the band had wanted to achieve something musically like Ayn Rand had in her novel "Anthem."

The original idea for attempting something as wide-reaching came from Neil Peart. He began working on lyrics and gradually his enthusiasm infected the other two members of the band. All told it took about six months for them to finish writing the material. Peart naturally concentrated on the lyrics and "musical suggestions" while Lee and Lifeson provided the music.

At the end of those six months Rush went into the Toronto Sound studios with producer/engineer Terry Brown and spent a month getting the completed work down on vinyl. It's worth noting, by the way, that '2112' like all their previous albums, was written by Rush while they were on the road. The recording contract they'd signed and the gruelling live touring schedule they'd set themselves allowed for very little time off.

Equally interesting, particularly when one hears the finished product, is that Rush used less overdubbing on '2112' than on any of their previous albums. They had learnt that it was important, if not essential, to be able to reproduce the studio sound of an album on stage – if they weren't going to run the risk of disappointing devoted fans.

As the title indicates the album is set in the future, in the year 2112, when the world is under the domination of a pseudo-religious dictatorship – the Priests of the Temple of Syrinx.

The Priests run society along the lines of benevolent and logical despotism. Anything which isn't logical has no place in society and must be destroyed.

It is, of course, portrayed as a soulless and joyless society devoid of any of the arts. The hero discovers an

ancient artefact – a guitar – which, to his amazement produces a curious hitherto unheard-of sound called music.

He takes his discovery to the Priests, convinced that they will be as thrilled as he is. But they conclude that music is illogical and can be of no earthly use and they destroy his guitar.

Miserably, the hero crawls away and has a dream about a world which is different from the one run by the Priests. This merely saddens him until he discovers that the planet of his dream is real and that things can change.

The close of the album with a god-like voice booming out "Attention all planets of the Solar Federation – we have assumed control . . . we have assumed control . . . we have assumed control" is one of the most chilling and powerful finales ever captured on vinyl. And on stage it's even better.

Needless to say, an album as controversial and as different as this has over the years caused a lot of polarised opinions.

Some critics have seen it as the ultimate example of Rush the raging right-wing capitalists. And matters weren't helped when Peart announced to one interviewer soon after the release of '2112' that he felt "humanitarians are just the same as dictators."

However, when the album was released, it proved to be very much Rush's breakthrough vinyl outing in the States. Billboard magazine described the album – rather curiously – as "Hard, crashing heavy metal rock from a trio that sounds like a lot of other groups but still stands out because of lead singer Geddy Lee's uncanny vocal resemblance to Robert Plant, and the better than average musicianship.

"Lots of fun – but the group, which has a large group of fans now, will need a bit more distinctive sound if they are to progress much more."

Cashbox reckoned that the album was a "valid and melodic tale of possible things to come" while *Record World* pronounced that '2112' was "an album sure to pass the Memorex test in 2112 or today."

As far as the band themselves were concerned '2112' was one hell of an achievement. Neil rated it as a first plateau, a realization of the aims the band had set themselves when they first got together. He also added a little later that the album had really drained Rush and had exhausted, temporarily, the band's supply of fresh ideas. That could have been the main reason why the next album from Rush was the tremendously exciting double live set 'All The World's A Stage' which came out in the autumn of 1976.

In June of that year Rush played three nights at Toronto's Massey Hall. Initially set to do just the 11th and 12th, the promoter, Martin Onret, had been forced to add a third night on the 13th to satisfy the colossal demand.

That should have been no surprise however. By the time June of that year had come round '2112' had sold 160,000 copies in North America. 'Rush' and 'Caress Of Steel' had received gold albums for sales in Canada and the band had completed a two month tour of the States playing well over 50 cities and headlining in most of them.

Apparently there was a colossal thunderstorm during the Rush stint at the Massey Hall with hailstones thundering out of the skies on to Toronto. But, judging by the sound that was recorded at those shows, Rush outdid the forces of nature. Peart just about demolished a drum kit in his frenetic efforts to get down a good sound.

The result of those three shows was the live album 'All The World's A Stage'. The band took the tapes of those concerts to their old familiar Toronto Sound studio and spent more than a month, working three or four days a week, remixing and dubbing. Fortunately, for those who believe that live albums really should be live and not some bastard offspring of the studio and the stage, Rush used very few overdubs on 'Stage'. Geddy Lee promised that there were just a couple of vocals dubs and a little judicious grafting of a drum solo from one night into the body of the performance from another. And there were technical details that had to be ironed out too, such as the fact that Alex Lifeson had broken a guitar string during 'Working Man' on one night which was corrected in the studio.

What 'Stage' represented, when it was released in September of 1976 was a kind of anthology of the band's best work from their first four albums.

In the States 'Stage' was the perfect follow-up to '2112' and garnered consistently good reviews. Just as an example, listen to *Record World* who said: "Building its American reputation slowly but steadily Rush stands poised for breaking through all the way via this two record live set reflecting the group's first four LPs and its North American tours of earlier this year. All the highly charged electricity is here in an explosive setting."

Surprisingly, though, like the previous four albums 'Stage' had still not been released in Britain. It was being imported in limited quantities by Phonogram Records who were still unsure of just how valid and worthwhile – commercially speaking – Rush were for the British market.

And, looking at it historically, you can see the record company's point. So-called "heavy metal" was just about the deadest dodo around, certainly as far as the majority of the media was concerned. New Wave was the thing and it would probably have seemed like the strangest thing in the world to actually start raving about a three piece "progressive" band from Canada – of all places. So Phonogram decided to follow a medium course and import Rush albums rather than release them in their own right.

However, it's a fact that they were watching out for signs that Rush could take off. Certainly sales of the import albums were doing exceptionally well. But there was also a certain gentleman by the name of Geoff Barton writing then – and now – for *Sounds* who was carrying on what was practically a one man crusade on behalf of Rush.

He got hold of a copy of 'All The World's A Stage' in November 1976 and gave it a rave review, rating it a five star album. He concluded a list of superlatives with the following advice: "Rush are probably the best undiscovered band in Britain at the moment. I strongly recommend you to check them out. Now."

In Canada punters were needing no such advice. By the end of the year 'Stage' had gone gold – the first home produced live album to go gold and the first double album to achieve that same feat.

During the autumn of 1976 Rush embarked on a coast to coast tour of their native Canada and then they followed this up with dates in the northwest of the United States and five dates in California.

Those latter dates give some indication of how Rush had grown in stature with the band pulling in a total of 45,000 people. Previously they had played just small club dates in the State.

At this stage Rush were in a rather

curious position as far as concert attendances were concerned in the United States. They were doing well in the West and the Midwest, able to play headline date after headline date at substantial concert halls. But in the east – areas like New York and Massachusetts – they had little pulling power at all. Given their intention to conquer the whole of the States, one way or another, Rush decided to chance their arms in the east during December 1976. They special guested with Foghat in New York and Massachusetts and in Montreal guested with Aerosmith.

In the stern city of Chicago way up in Illinois Rush had previously managed to bring in just 1,400 people. In December of 1976 they headlined in a 4,000 seater hall – a date which had sold out two weeks in advance.

In Indianapolis, one of Rush's strong territories, the band headlined a three act show – Bob Seger and The Atlanta Rhythm Section opened – and they drew in a spectacular 18,000 people.

On December 30 in Hamilton, Ontario, Rush played before 3,300 – a capacity crowd – with 2,000 more people being turned away in sub-zero temperatures. The band sold out their New Year's Eve show at the Toronto Concert Bowl within a few days and they had to add a second date at the same venue – also sold out – on January 3, 1977. More than 14,000 people paid to get into these shows which confirmed Rush as the top-drawing live rock band in Canada.

The year of 1977 opened up in much the same way as 1976 closed with Rush out on the road gigging everywhere between Houston, Texas and Pittsburgh, Pennsylvania. However, there was a new feeling of confidence within the band. They'd been picking up gold albums all over the place and had expanded their sphere of live operations to cover the whole of the North American continent. Said Alex Lifeson at the end of 1976: "We seem to have been on the road for four years and occasionally get the odd day off." He admitted that it was just about impossible to break down their schedule into separate tours. All of the dates seemed to run into each other.

But in 1977 they were planning well ahead and giving themselves more time to work on their albums – instead of having to write them in the spare time that they had on the road.

One of their plans for the future which they announced at the end of 1976 was that they would be coming to Britain in the middle of 1977 to record their next album. Fans in Britain reasoned that if that were so the odds were that Rush would also be playing some live dates – their first outside of North America.

The decision to try recording in England was an interesting one. The band had never recorded outside of Toronto, at least not successfully. At the end of 1976 they'd tried working in New York's Electric Lady Studios – the operation set up by the late Jimi Hendrix and immortalised on his 'Electric Ladyland' album with its notorious British cover. However they'd been forced to scrap what they'd done simply because they were dissatisfied with the results. One of the reasons was apparently that they didn't feel at home in an American studio – curious, since they were spending most of their time in the States at this stage.

Favourite studio for the new album, at the time, appeared to be George Martin's AIR Studios in London's Oxford Street. Easily one of the best appointed in the country it would have been a natural choice. Also it would have been something of a spiritual home-coming for Neil Peart since the last time he'd been in London he'd been working a stone's throw away in Carnaby Street selling trinkets to the tourists.

As it turned out, however, Rockfield Studios in South Wales were to get Rush's custom and the album they recorded there was the excellent 'A Farewell To Kings.' But that's getting ahead of ourselves. Before Rockfield beckoned Rush had a lot more dates to get through.

In January of 1977 they were being raved over in Houston, Texas by the local rock critic who drooled over the band's music and reckoned that Rush were "in rare and esteemed company."

In Columbus, Ohio, the band had originally scheduled one concert but that sold out within a week and a second one was added. The local writer there on the *Columbus Dispatch* seemed astounded that "heavy metal rock" was still popular. "Wrapping up", she wrote, "anyone who braved snow and winds to experience the show were far more than warmed up. They were fried to a frizzle by Rush."

At the same time, though, most critics were talking about how Rush had gotten where they were without much, if any, radio airplay which previously had been reckoned as being essential to any sort of success for a rock band in the States.

And this was a factor that was worrying the band's American record company too. It was, they figured, all very well for Rush to be slogging their guts out in every gig that God sent but radio airplay would be very much the icing on the cake, a way of reaching far more rock fans than if Rush stayed on the road until hell froze over.

So they came up with a plan. Phonogram/Mercury decided to put together a special sampler album for rock radio stations featuring tracks from the last three Rush studio albums. In addition they set up an extensive advertising campaign for all five of the band's albums.

Said one Jules Abramson, senior vice president of marketing: "We are zeroing in on the entire Rush catalogue of albums because we feel once a person sees the group in concert or hears a recent LP they will want other albums by

:he group."

The sampler album was cunningly entitled 'Everything Your Listeners Ever Wanted To Hear By Rush ... But You Were Afraid To Play.' It featured five tracks from 'Fly By Night,' three from 'Caress Of Steel' and four from '2112.'

A promotion man for the company added that "Sometimes radio programmers' tastes do not coincide with their listeners'. For example, both Aerosmith and Kiss were forced on the air by listeners. And now it's Rush. "A group of this nature can easily go from gold to platinum status with airplay."

Whether the record company's scheme had any real effect it's difficult to say even now. The first time I spoke with Rush, Geddy and Neil were both resigned to the seeming fact that they would never get any radio airplay.

Geddy told me: "As far as we're concerned it seems that radio programmers don't believe we exist. No matter how many sell-out shows we do, no matter how many albums we sell they still don't seem to be interested.

"I don't think there's any point in being bitter about it, though. It seems to be just a fact of life. As long as we keep pulling in audiences and selling records we believe that we're doing the right thing. Anyway, we've been on the road for so long now I don't think we could imagine any other kind of lifestyle."

Even as late as May 1981, Rolling Stone magazine was still commenting on "radio station programme directors who deem the group's brand of progressive aggro-rock as unfit for airplay."

Between April 8 and May 21 Rush played a series of American dates concentrating mainly on the north east – their weakest area – plus a few midwest dates. They opened in Toledo, Ohio, and closed in Chicago with two nights at the Aragaon Ballroom.

After a short break the band geared themselves up for their first European tour. The first three dates were scheduled for Britain – Manchester Free Trade Hall on June 2, Birmingham Odeon on June 3 and London Hammersmith Odeon on June 4.

They were then set to play dates in Sweden, Germany and Holland, all of which countries boasted a small but vociferous cult following for Rush – usually propagated by word of mouth.

There was quiet confidence in the Rush camp about the upcoming dates – but significantly in Britain tickets for the three shows were put on sale well up front (about seven weeks ahead as a matter of fact).

Of course, they sold out within days. To appreciate the significance of that achievement you have to remember that this was the summer of '77. The Clash were singing 'London's Burning' and The Sex Pistols were finding it hard to get anywhere to play at all – and getting maximum publicity out of their predicament.

Rush seemed about as at home in this musical maelstrom as the Duke of Edinburgh would be at the Marquee. And yet they thrived.

The biggest surprise among the British rock critics appeared to be that a band like Rush came from Canada. Writer Dave Redshaw who reviewed Rush's Manchester date recalls his astonishment that Canada – land of Joni Mitchell and The Band – could cough up anything like Rush.

Redshaw zeroed in on the band's affection for Ayn Rand – a decidedly unfashionable stance in the punk days – and also likened Geddy's singing voice to that of David Surkamp of the relatively obscure Pavlov's Dog, a comparison that was to be repeated many times in the British rock press over the next few years.

What was highly important about those first dates in Britain was that it was obvious that Rush, despite little if any promotion, had sufficient fans for them to sell out major venues up and down the country.

In addition, those fans were sufficiently loyal to have searched out the Rush albums that were available in this country on import. As Redshaw recalls "They seemed to know every single riff that Rush played."

With those dates to their credit, plus the European ones which went equally well, Rush hightailed it to the wilds of South Wales and Rockfield Studios. They were to begin work on an album which had the working title of 'Closer To The Heart.' When it was finally released in September of 1977 it had been renamed 'A Farewell To Kings.'

True to their word Rush, having described 'All The World's A Stage' as the end of the beginning, the closer to Phase One, brought out an experimental and refreshing album in the shape of 'A Farewell To Kings.'

There was certainly a pastoral feeling to some of the tracks – perhaps due to the bucolic surroundings of Rockfield – but the band also seemed more relaxed and more sure of their capabilities.

They also included a blockbuster of a track in the shape of 'Cygnus X-1' which culminates in the spacecraft pilot hero plunging into a Black Hole – a neat science fiction version of the cliffhanger endings of the old Saturday matinée movies. Would he return? And how? And How!

Rush did some extra work on the 'Farewell' album at Advision Studios in the heart of London's West End – a setting which couldn't have been further from Rockfield.

And at the time I had just become press officer for the band at Phonogram in London. We were all aware at the record company that we had a potentially hot property on our hands in the form of Rush and it was up to me to pull in some press coverage on them.

On July 13 I found myself in the company of *Melody Maker's* Chris Welch heading for Advision in a limo. We were ushered into the presence and I said a few small words of introduction before making myself scarce. There's a code of conduct in interviews which means that you should never really sit in on a discussion between a journalist and an artist. You might cramp both their styles and end up with a very stilted interview.

I went to see Rush again – if only to make myself vaguely known to them – a couple of days later. I decided I should take a few beers with me to make myself more welcome.

I was greeted politely and we talked of this and that, but inevitably it was all small talk and somehow I found myself getting more and more embarrassed. It was obvious that they wanted to get on with what they were doing – pressure of time and all that – so I left Rush and Terry Brown to their own devices and scurried off.

I remember thinking that they were kind of stand-offish people and wondering what it was that had made things so unnatural and uncomfortable.

I realized later – much later – that Rush collectively have the most immense power of concentration. They apply themselves to one task at a time devoting all their time and energy to it until it is complete. I said at the beginning of this book that the opening of their British tour in February 1978, was when I first met them. So even though I had encountered them at

Advision more than six months earlier I still feel that that tour was the first time I met them.

At the beginning of August a tape arrived at Phonogram's London offices – a tape of the new album, 'A Farewell To Kings.' A playback of the album was arranged, a record company tradition which allows the people who'll be working on the album to get used to it before it's released and to work out just how to present the album when they're approaching record company executives or music paper journalists.

We decided that this was the ideal opportunity to give Geoff Barton of *Sounds* an exclusive upfront preview of the album. He had been easily the staunchest supporter of Rush in Britain since their albums had started trickling over and besides that we figured that if we gave him an exclusive we'd get better and bigger coverage of the album. It's a standard record company ploy.

But Barton wasn't to be found. He was on holiday or on the road with someone – or something like that. So we opted for *Sounds'* Pete Makowski, second only to Barton in enthusiasm for Rush.

He duly turned up to the playback at Phonogram on August 4 at 6.30 pm and we all settled down to listen. Disaster was just round the corner. One side of the playback quipment broke down and it was a ood 15 minutes before anyone realised hat we were hearing a muted, sort of trangled version of 'A Farewell.' I got erbally murdered by my boss but Aakowski was more than generous and eld nothing against me.

The album was finally released vorldwide in September 1977. This was he first time that a Rush album had een released in its own right in the UK t the same time as in the States. When t came out Rush were starting yet nother American tour – but in Britain 'honogram were doing their utmost to break" the album, blitzing the media in very way they could think of.

Through a combination of the rilliance of the album and the promot- onal push 'Farewell' began to sell in itherto unknown quantities.

In the States in November three lbums were certified gold on the same lay – '2112', 'All The World's A Stage' nd 'A Farewell To Kings'. The speed vith which the latter sold is some ndication of just how much Rush had rown in America.

At the end of 1977 it was announced hat Rush would be playing a 16-date our of Britain. The stampede to the box ffices was colossal and every ticket was old out two months ahead of the first late on the tour – Birmingham Odeon n February 12, 1978.

The British dates were, in fact, along vith the American tour which began in September 1977, part of Rush's "A Farewell To Kings" world tour. It ended n June 1978 by which time the band had ttracted well over one million concert- oers to their shows.

As I said before, that British tour vas one of the most startling, the most evelatory I'd ever seen. The band's laying was consistently immaculate, he sound crystal clear and the light how was quite unlike anything I'd seen efore.

The lights were operated by Rush's ighly experienced tour manager, Ioward Ungerleider who had been with hem before Neil Peart joined.

I first met him a few days before the Rush tour of '78. Ungerleider, product manager Alan Phillips and myself had dinner at a restaurant near Marble Arch, mulling over various problems or events which were likely to arise on the tour. I was there probably just to make up the numbers since it was Phillips and Ungerleider who had the real responsi- bility.

Ungerleider, a heavyweight in size but a true gentleman in character told us story after story about his tour managing career. One that I recall is when he was looking after (I believe) Savoy Brown and they were taking a domestic flight in the States. Ungerleider glanced out of the window and noticed a pair of trousers flashing by, followed closely by shirts and other miscellaneous objects. Someone had forgotten to batten down the cargo door and half the band's gear took a solo flight.

On all the occasions I met Ungerleider I'd never seen him flustered – no mean achievement considering the amount of gear the band carted round and the heavy responsibility which rested on Ungerleider's shoulders.

But then Ungerleider made sure that he had good people around him too – particularly the magnificently named Lurch who was about seven feet tall, pretty well-built but the original gentle giant. Lurch's cross in life was the fact that every time the band toured outside of the States he knew he'd have to resign himself to beds which were around a foot too short for him. One of the great pluses about Lurch was that he had only to walk into a room and any trouble makers around would do a double take and instantly quieten down.

Throughout that tour it was evident that the band and the road crew were essentially a happy family – corny and clichéd I know, but true. Unlike many other bands that could be mentioned, Peart, Lee and Lifeson never seemed to "pull rank" on any members of their crew.

During that tour I came to learn that Rush were unfailingly polite. Occasion- ally interviewers from the local press would fail to show up which usually meant a long wait in a cold room somewhere in the bowels of a theatre. But I don't recall the band ever complaining.

The nearest any of them came to it was when I set up a couple of interviews before a show. Neil did both of them then suggested afterwards in a quiet and reasonable tone of voice that he would prefer interviews to take place after shows – he needed the time beforehand to psyche himself up.

They also seemed willing to talk about any subject. In Newcastle I took Robin Smith from *Record Mirror* to see the show and do an interview afterwards. There in the Holiday Inn – which is situated miles out of town in a place suitably called Wideopen – Robin settled down to talk to the band. He noticed there were several radio controlled model cars lying around the room and started asking about them.

As I left him with the band Neil was merrily nattering on about how one of Rush's favourite occupations was to race these little cars around venues during soundchecks.

Rush were due to play two nights at Hammersmith Odeon on this tour on Sunday and Monday, February 19 and 20. One of the stunts that Phonogram had planned was to fly an enormous hot air balloon over Hammersmith with Rush emblazoned all over it. Sadly, the balloon, piloted by a really nice guy by the name of Mike Glue, wouldn't get off

he ground from its launching site in Battersea Park on the Sunday.

However, to borrow a phrase, the balloon really did go up the following day – thanks to *NME* writer Miles. The band had agreed to do a series of interviews at their hotel, the Holiday Inn, Marble Arch on Monday. One of the journalists to turn up was Miles – a highly rated and highly respected writer by anyone's standards.

I introduced him to Neil Peart and left the two of them in spirited discussion. One of the topics they strayed on to was Rush's political philosophy and their fascination with the anti-collectivism of Ayn Rand.

A week later the interview appeared in *NME*. I glanced at it, noting that it was quite long and then put the magazine down to read at my leisure. A few minutes later product manager Alan Phillips came into my office holding the *NME* and asking in a choked voice "Have you seen this?" I picked up my copy of the paper and read it through rapidly. Miles had taken Rush to be little more than a bunch of crypto-fascists and he was issuing stern warnings against the desirability of such a band playing in public.

I was aghast. And later when Peart and the rest of the band read it they joined me in that emotion. Of course, there's no doubt that Miles wrote it as he saw it and there was no question of a deliberate axe job but all the same the results looked pretty damning in print.

Eventually the fuss died down. And, while Peart still remembers the piece and the interview vividly, he tends not to talk about it any more. In a curious way I think Miles' article helped to establish the band somehow.

I suppose it's just another case of there being no such thing as bad publicity – however corny that may sound.

Aside from that piece the papers tended to be very enthusiastic about Rush and their show. All in all it was fair to say that Rush had broken through in Britain.

To help establish them even further Phonogram released a low price three record set consisting of the band's first three albums and called 'Archives'. It achieved extremely healthy sales.

At the end of their world tour Rush found themselves back home in Canada where they were honoured with a second Juno Award, this time for "best group of the year."

After a short break the band came back to Britain and they hightailed it down to Rockfield studios again to work on their new album. It was finished off in London at Advision and Trident Studios.

The new album was called 'Hemispheres' and, in hindsight, it seems reasonable to suppose that Rush felt pressure upon themselves to bring out both an outstanding and different album. After all, in Canada they had earned three platinum albums and three gold, while in the States they were riding on three gold.

'Hemispheres' was released in October 1978, and by the time December rolled round it had already gone gold in the States.

'Hemispheres' was probably Rush's most ambitious album to date. It was originally inspired by a book called 'Powers Of Mind' written by Adam Smith. Neil Peart explained that Smith was a researcher who studied the occult and various other kinds of philosophies, tried LSD, transcendental meditation and so on.

Smith devotes one chapter in his book to the division of the brain into hemispheres – Apollo being the right hand side of the brain and Dionysius the left.

Side one of 'Hemispheres' is devoted to the further adventures of Cygnus, the character who was last seen in 'A Farewell To Kings', plummeting through a Black Hole in his spaceship Rocinante.

Says Peart who, of course, wrote the lyrics for the album: "The world he leaves is being ruled over by two gods who represent opposing forces – Apollo and Dionysius. Apollo champions the force of reason and rationale and Dionysius champions the force of instinct and intuition. I'm taking the setting back to the dawn of creation when there was just man not knowing who he is or why he's there.

"Apollo comes along and gives the people a shot at progress and offers all these benefits and they say 'sure we'd like fires to warm us in winter'.

"They follow him along and build amazing cities and get involved in science and build beautiful things just for the sake of it. But they're bored because they don't have an emotional attachment to the things that they're making. They lose the knack and the interest in doing them any more. An ennui falls over everybody and they hang out, bored.

"They go after Dionysius who tells them what he can offer and obviously it's the instinctive and artistic side of things that he offers them – the music and dancing and love. They say 'yeah, that sounds great after what we've had'.

"Everyone has a wonderful time, they leave the cities and just rave. But when winter comes along they've lost the skills that would keep them warm and that whole rational side of them doesn't function the way it did. So the wolves and cold get to them and at that point they break into total anarchy and chaos. That's the Armageddon section of the song because both Apollo and Dionysis are fighting for control."

Eventually the whole problem is solved by the arrival of Cygnus. He points out the chaos that the struggle between Apollo and Dionysius is causing. So they appoint him as a god – the bringer of balance.

Essentially it's a classic Rush theme. Peart seems to have a horror of human stupidity and is forever preaching that the middle ground is the only way to go.

Thus, in 'Hemispheres' there's also a track called 'The Trees' which is about what would happen to oaks and maples should they ever act as stupidly as people do. It can be read as a union-bashing song but I think that only diminishes what Peart is saying – peaceful co-existence and live and let live are all.

There are just two other tracks on 'Hemispheres'. 'Circumstances' deals with disillusion while 'La Villa Strangiato' is an instrumental, reckoned by the band to be a musical reflection of some of the strange dreams that Alex Lifeson is prey to. The latter piece is also subtitled 'An Exercise In Self Indulgence' which rather gives the lie to those people who imagine that Rush are a humourless and over-pretentious band.

'Hemispheres' proved not to be exactly everyone's cup of tea. Geoff Barton in *Sounds,* with commendable honesty, announced that he couldn't make up his mind whether the album

was the greatest or the worst thing that Rush had done.

And the *NME,* in a convoluted and verbose review – which lumped in 'Hemispheres' with Art Bears 'Hopes And Fears' and Funkadelic's 'One Nation Under A Groove' – found the Rush philosophy "frightening." However, the fans appeared to have no such reticence. 'Hemispheres' probably more than any other Rush album brought the band in touch with a much wider audience.

Up till then they were still regarded as very much in the symphonic end of the heavy metal mainstream. 'Hemispheres' seemed to make the band an appealing prospect to the thousands of Yes and Genesis fans throughout the country.

When the album was released in October Rush started on their 'Hemispheres' world tour which was to last until June the following year and see the band playing a startling total of 113 dates in Canada, the States, Britain and Europe. In December 1978, 'Hemispheres' went gold in the States and in the same month Rush played three nights at the Maple Leaf Gardens in Toronto setting an indoor Canadian attendance record.

RUSH
pearl
RUSH
pearl

In the middle of January Rush played two nights at the prestigious New York Palladium. It's not a massive venue by north east American rock and roll standards but to play there is recognized as an important plateau in a rock band's career.

Their dates there were reviewed by John Rockwell, the influential rock critic of the New York Times – the first occasion, I believe, when their existence was acknowledged by this particular august organ.

Rockwell didn't exactly go overboard for Rush but like most of his predecessors, who went into the band's concerts knowing not a great deal about them and having no particular enthusiasm for their style of music, he emerged showing respect for the trio.

He opened his review by commenting that rock critics spend much of their time "splashing about in the new wave, but an occasional dunking in the old wave probably wouldn't harm them any." He then dismissed the concepts of old and new waves, commented on the size and the enthusiasm of the crowd at their Palladium dates and added "even if Rush feels a bit miffed about the way it's ignored by the supposed taste-makers of rock, it can take consolation in its audience's enthusiasm.

"What Rush does is play tight, energetic progressive rock with a strong science fiction overlay." Through being a three piece, said Rockwell, Rush kept its music uncluttered and unfussy unlike so many other science fantasy bands.

He approved of the complexity of the parts played by Alex and Neil and added "Mr Lee sings in a spare but unusual way – a brittle androgynous tenor."

To his own taste Rockwell found Rush a little "busy and empty in the manner of too many of these souped-up, neo-King Crimson outfits.

"But there can be no denying that Rush answers some sort of need, and answers it with crisp, professional dispatch."

Not exactly a rave review but one which showed respect and a deal of understanding about what Rush were attempting to do and the numbers of people who appreciated what Rush were doing. Although the review doesn't exactly rate alongside the conversion of Saul on the road to Tarsus it was the kind of press that Rush needed at the

time. They were still being ignored by the radio station people in the States at the time so coverage by well-read and respected journals was essential alongside, of course, the massive turnouts that they were getting in concert halls across North America.

In the February edition of Circus magazine Alex Lifeson found himself promoted to the status of a first division "heavy metal axeman" while Rush themselves were described as "Canada's premier pulverizers". The writer was David Fricke, a long-time chronicler of Rush's activities in various journals, who had decided that Lifeson, with the exception of Eddie Van Halen and Ted Nugent, was the most charismatic and talented heavy metal guitarist North America had produced.

Said Fricke: "Lifeson has developed a working heavy metal style that, unlike his flagging contemporaries, isn't all power chords and decibels.

"The extended instrumental 'La Villa Strangiato' (from 'Hemispheres') showcases that style with an impressive technical display of not only his playing but how well he shoulders the responsibility of filling melodic and harmonic holes in a three piece format."

Fricke later quotes Geddy Lee saying (of Alex): "Yeah he's got a lot of weight on his shoulders but no more than Neil and I. For our music to work we have to have a rhythm section that's always happening. And that's what sets us apart from other power trios – we have a lot happening in the rhythm section, lots of changes, even melodies."

The second week in February saw Sounds magazine in England announcing a "Rush, Nugent, Aerosmith Blitzkrieg" – which was another way of saying that they'd got wind of projected British tours planned by these three acts. Rush, they said, were scheduled to play more than 15 dates in 10 cities in England and Scotland – but dates were to be confirmed. They added that Rush had been touring America extensively since the release of 'Hemispheres' in November.

A week later the news was confirmed. The band was set for 18 dates during April and May of 1979 – three nights at London's Hammersmith Odeon, two apiece at Newcastle, Glasgow, Manchester, Liverpool, Birmingham and Bristol and one-offs at Edinburgh, Coventry and Southampton. The original plan was for them to do 36

NATIONAL
LORTON, VA.

FRIENDLY

CLEANER'S
SHOE SERVICE

dates, such was the demand by fans, but the band felt that they couldn't cope with such a large addition to an already exhausting schedule which they had set themselves.

After all, apart from Britain the band were also lined up to play dates in Germany, Holland, Norway, Sweden, Belgium and Finland in a six week sell-out tour.

Eventually, the number of nights they ended up playing at Hammersmith Odeon was five – a remarkable achievement for any band. Incidentally, before they set off for the tour they were awarded yet another Juno in Canada for being "Best Group Of The Year" and when they got to London they were presented with a silver disc for sales in Britain of 'A Farewell To Kings'.

I paid a flying visit to Glasgow on April 25 to see Rush playing the presti-gious Glasgow Apollo. It was very much a Canadian night out in the massive but run-down Scottish venue with Rush protegés Max Webster opening the show.

It was the first visit to Europe for The Websters and it was only natural that they should be accompanying Rush since they all grew up together. Moreover they shared the same management company.

Max Webster: Kim Mitchell (guitar and vocals), Dave Myles (bass), Terry Watkinson (keyboards), Gary McCracken (drums) and Pye Dubois (lyricist and fifth member of the band, without actually ever appearing with them on stage), had been in existence since 1973, having originally been formed by Mitchell and Dubois.

They'd signed with Mercury, the record company who also looked after Rush, but had suffered in comparison. Mitchell and Dubois had told me earlier that week that Rush had been very much the favoured sons as far as Mercury had been concerned while Max Webster had been treated as second best.

"But Rush themselves turned out to be a real help to us. We toured with them a couple of times in America," said Mitchell "and they were terrific. They helped us to play in front of a lot more people than we might have expected."

By the time The Websters came to

the UK in 1979 they had switched to another record company, Capitol, who were pulling out all the stops to impress. Perhaps they had a weather eye on Rush, in the hope that their contract with Phonogram was soon to expire. Whatever, Capitol did their best for Max Webster and, at the time, I recorded that they played a fine and imaginative set which, given a degree of justice in the world, would have gone a long way to establishing them in Britain.

But, at the same time, I also went on record as saying that at the Apollo – and, as it turned out, everywhere else – the night belonged to Rush.

They had rarely been in such magnificent form, made all the more impressive by the fact that all three of the Rush guys had succumbed to heavy colds within hours of touching down in Britain.

As usual, the light show was magnificent which meant that Rush had to do their usual outstanding job as far as the musical side of the evening was concerned.

They not only achieved that, but in actual fact surpassed it. Despite the fact that they played for more than two hours, despite the fact that we all stood for the whole of that time, despite the heat, the overpowering volume, the smoke, the lack of oxygen – despite all this by the time the band had left the stage for the last time I felt as though they'd played for about five minutes. I could see people all round me looking as though they shared that impression. Heads shaken from side to side as though they'd just come out of a trance, people sneaking glances at watches and adopting weird expressions of surprise.

Rush had incorporated a substantial chunk of 'Hemispheres' into their set, alongside standards and gems from earlier albums.

The set included 'Anthem', 'By-Tor And The Snow Dog', 'Xanadu', 'The Trees', 'Cygnus X-1', 'Hemispheres', 'La Villa Strangiato', 'Bangkok', 'Twilight Zone', 'Something For Nothing', the full '2112', 'Working Man', 'Bastille Day', and 'In The Mood'.

Reviews in the music press varied. *Melody Maker* and *Sounds* were decidedly approving, while *Record Mirror* were less than enthusiastic, a publication called *Popstar Weekly* ended their "review" with the slogan "Canucks go home" and *NME* reacted predictably.

One Glenn Gibson declared Rush "riddled with unforgiveable faults" and concluded that "During any lull in the explosions and whirling lights the band seemed as though they'd be booed off in a pub. That was the only time you ever noticed them."

Gibson's critical premise seemed based on the fact that Rush placed an awful lot of stress on visual effects and, as such, were fair game for castigation. On the one side declaring the overall effect as "almost awe-inspiring", Gibson tempered this almost grudging praise with the suggestion since Rush had enough money to hire the best people in the world to provide these visual effects they were guaranteed to come up with "some worthy aspects to the show."

A confused review, but one indicative of the critical climate at the time, which tended to be almost unanimous in the view that anyone like Clash was ideologically pure and therefore their music was wonderful, whereas as someone like Rush – definitely politically suspect – automatically had to come out with duff music.

If the present reader feels that many critics of the time got their only exercise from jumping to conclusions he wouldn't be too far off the mark.

If only *NME's* Gibson had known Rush had plans to make the eye-dazzling parts of their show even more supernova. At the time Neil Peart told me that the intention was for Rush to treat their British fans to the nearest thing they could manage to their North American touring set-up, given the vastly different sizes of the venues they played either side of the Atlantic.

One thing the British fans hadn't seen which the North Americans had, was the Rush back-projection show: this was to come later, during the 'Moving Pictures' tour in 1981.

"We put everything back into our road show" Peart told me "because we know how important it is to keep up the excitement of a live show. The back projection is just another way of keeping up that excitement, along with the lights and all that.

"We know there are some parts of

our set which aren't quite as musically active as others so the best thing to do there is to make sure that attention is centred on stage.

"There's no question of the effects taking anything away from the music – it's a question of highlighting, or illustrating it."

During the interviews they gave on the British tour Rush revealed that 'Hemispheres' had taken them much longer to record than any other album they'd been involved in – two and a half months of recording alone at Rockfield before they even got down to mixing at Trident.

Alex Lifeson explained one of the reasons was that it had been the most "arranged" of all their albums which, paradoxically, meant that since they ha[d] a clearer idea of what they wanted to do it took them longer to achieve exactly that result.

They had planned to spend just on six weeks recording 'Hemispheres' but, as Peart pointed out, at the same time a[s] they had progressed through their mus[i]cal career, they had become more exacting in their demands upon themselves.

He told one interviewer: "Our standards are very high. Second best isn't good enough."

In addition, while they were here, th

nd and their management let slip a
uple of reminders to the media to
ow that it still wasn't easy going for
ish in Britain, or most other places for
at matter, as far as mass media
ceptance was concerned. The band
ere very big among the public of quite
few countries around the world but
ess and radio were still taking a
utious view of them.

Co-manager Ray Danniels said,
mparing the Max Webster and Rush
tuation: "The press have gone for Max
ebster straight away yet Rush has
en a band they have seemed to want to
oid." He added hastily, however, "But it
esn't affect the band."

Alex Lifeson, when asked if he'd read the British reviews of 'Hemispheres' said that he'd only read Geoff Barton's in *Sounds* and hadn't seen the ones in *MM* or *NME* because "They don't like us very much anyway." Even then he probably hadn't derived too much joy from Geoff's since the latter had indicated his own personal confusion over 'Hemispheres' feeling it was either a masterpiece or a terrible mistake.

To his credit Barton subsequently stated that he stood by what he said in the 'Hemispheres' review but added he was probably pretty much alone in his opinion and that that particular album had bust Rush's potential market wide

open, bringing the Yes-type fans alongside the masses of heavy metal fanatics.

Aside from that the point remains that Rush's coverage in the papers and their exposure on radio in no way reflected their enormous popularity. By now, however, I believe even that didn't really bother the three very much. They had succeeded despite being ignored and were now in a position to ignore the pundits.

Happily, they never did. From the first day I met them until now they have always been unfailingly polite towards the rock press and enormously helpful. And they still maintain their strict rota of doing interviews in turn.

Anyway, back to the narrative. After the British dates Rush headed for the Continent where they were due to open a European tour in Paris, on May 15. Unfortunately the hall burnt down – fortunately before they'd got there – so that was rescheduled. The band opened in Belgium and went on through Germany, Switzerland, Denmark, Sweden and Norway. That series went on until the middle of June, 1979. Then it was back to Canada for a break – their first since October of the previous year and the first for more than 150 concerts.

However, within a month of their getting back home, it was announced in the music papers that Rush would be coming back to the UK to do a one-off show at the massive, barn-like Stafford Bingley Hall on September 21. The reason, according to the papers, was that Rush were planning to record their next album in the UK – the betting was on Trident in London as the favoured studio – and that they would take the opportunity to play a special concert here.

There had been such an overwhelming demand for tickets on the previous visit that Rush felt they should give the fans who had missed them a chance to see the band – and the people surrounding Rush obviously felt highly confident they'd have no trouble filling the 10,000 plus capacity hall.

No trouble? Too right – because within a week of the date being announced it had been sold out and the promoters, Straight Music, quickly

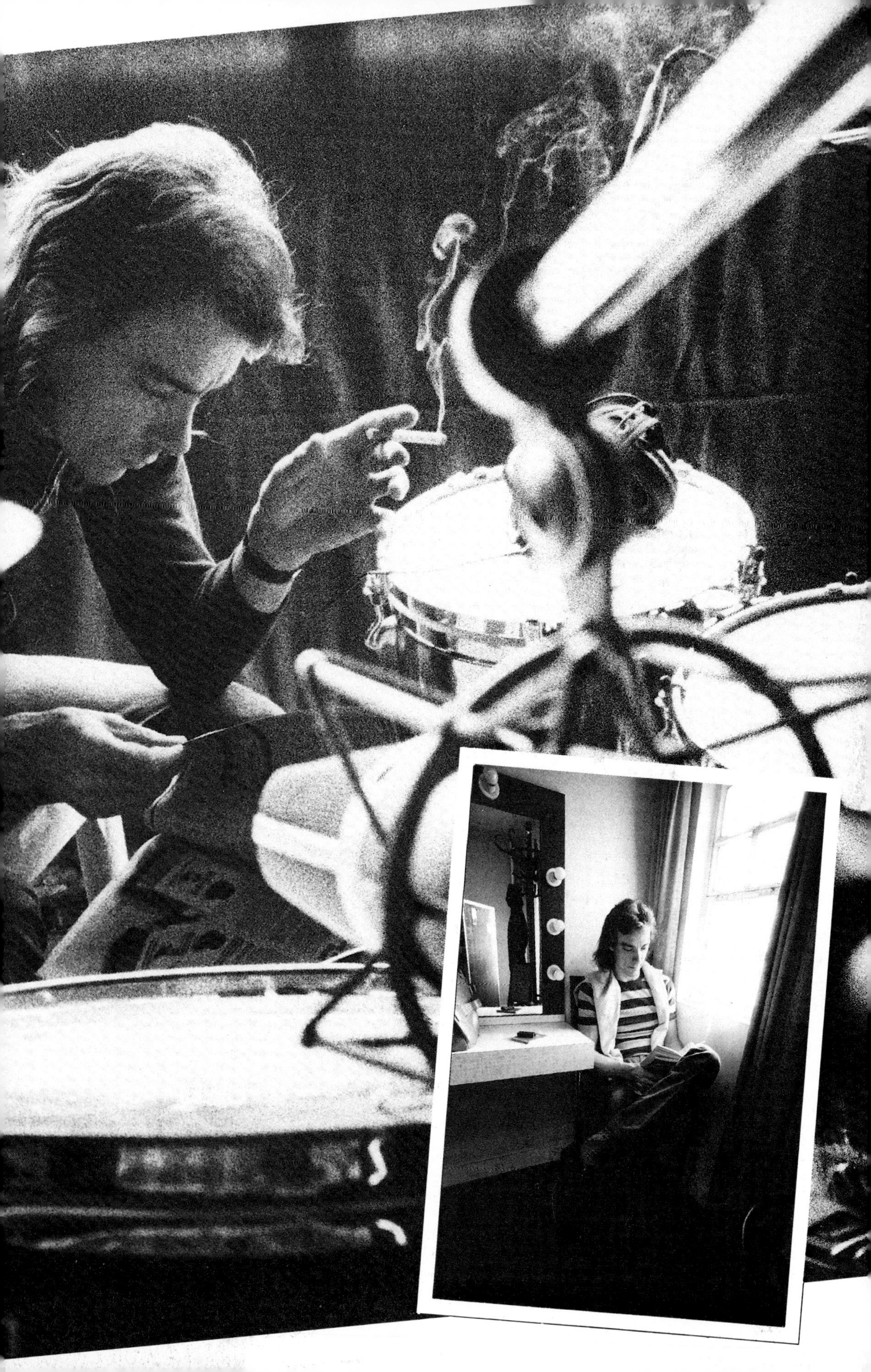

organised another one for the following night. All in all 20,000 tickets sold without too much trouble at all – if anyone needed confirmation that Rush were a major act they had only to look at those figures.

However, those shows were still in the future and in the meantime Rush were taking a well-earned rest before settling down to work on new material for the upcoming album. This was a deliberate and conscious change for Rush compared with their previous style of doing things. In effect this had been a question of touring just about all the time and taking the long dead hours that every band endures on tour – travelling, sitting in hotel rooms etc. – to use as writing time.

For the new album – 'Permanent Waves', as it turned out to be titled – Rush moved themselves off to a place called Lakewoods Farm in Ontario where Peart locked himself away in a cottage, adjoining the farm, and got down to work on the lyrics. While he was beavering away in splendid isolation Lifeson was playing about with his guitars and Geddy was accustoming himself to his ever burgeoning collection of instruments, mainly electronic.

The first thing that they actually cobbled together was an instrumental given the intriguing nonsense title of 'Uncle Tounous' – basically a workout of different ideas and a testing ground for musical effects. You won't find 'Uncle Tounous' on any album. Instead it was what one might consider as a prototype, ideas which were incorporated into, or formed the basis for, a whole collection of different songs and tunes.

First to be finished were 'Spirit Of Radio', 'Free Will' and 'Jacob's Ladder'. These songs, and others from 'Waves' were to be dusted off on dates that the band had fixed up for around the same time as the recording for the album, including the British dates at Stafford.

The track on the album which took the longest time was 'Natural Science'. Rush had finished doing the demos for everything on the album except one track. They had moved from Lakewoods Farm to Le Studio in Montreal to begin recording in earnest, but there was still that gap.

For a while it looked as though something Neil had been working on, based on the medieval epic 'Sir Gawain & The Green Knight' might fill the gap, but it wasn't to be.

"It became too out of place with the album's other material", explained Neil "so the project was shelved. But this did leave us with a gaping hole in the LP's plan. So while Alex and Geddy worked on overdubs I secluded myself to try to write something.

"For two days I stared in frustration at blank sheets of paper but on the third day something began to take shape, eventually taking the form of 'Natural Science', the album's concluding track."

The album was mixed at Trident on their British jaunt and it was eventually released in January, 1980. Two of the album's songs, 'Spirit Of Radio' and 'Free Will' were heard for the first time in the UK at the Bingley Hall shows and significantly, the former received a tumultuous response. Almost on a par, in fact, with the classic 'Farewell To Kings'. The show that I went to – the first – was a complete and utter triumph for the band. I'm told by others who went to the second show that that one went equally well.

The band played for about two hours each night, punctuating their show with their spectacular light show. By the time it was over that first night the crowd filed out in an almost reverent fashion, as though they'd been witnesses to a religious experience, more than a rock concert.

To support the release of 'Permanent Waves' Rush fixed up an exhausting tour schedule – as usual – which was set to cover most of North America from January through until the middle part of May. A European tour was mooted to begin in May.

With the album released in January, tickets went on sale for dates throughout Canada and the United States. On the record front the band enjoyed spectacular success with 'Permanent Waves' spiralling up the album charts and eventually making Top Five in the three majors – *Billboard, Cashbox* and *Record World.*

In Britain it made number three. However, as heartening as those performances were to the band, its record company and management, they must ave been absolutely stunned by the way e single, 'Spirit Of Radio', exploded orldwide. For the first time ever Rush ad a genuine, certified worldwide hit ngle. A few weeks earlier David Fricke *Circus* magazine had recorded this tle scenario, which illustrates all the ore starkly how Rush had done eviously with singles.

"The disc jockey at CHOM-FM, Iontreal, is winding up a radio terview with Geddy Lee, singer and ass guitarist with Rush. Ploughing esperately through a pile of Rush bums on the floor, while the last record des out, he finally looks at Lee with a ervous smile. 'Let's go out with a hit'."

"A hit?" Lee looks genuinely puzzled. Ve don't have any hits."

But a hit they did have with 'Spirit Of adio' and, of course, with 'Permanent 'aves' which indicated that the long ard years of slogging around were aying off in a major way. On the concert ont this kind of acceptance was being emonstrated in a spectacular fashion roughout North America with sell-uts being reported within hours of ckets going on sale and shows being dded on all over the place.

The fervour for Rush was very nearly demonstrated in tragic fashion in Detroit in January. A month previously – December 3 to be exact – 11 fans had been illed in Riverfront Stadium in incinnati when the crowd rushed the ates at a Who concert.

Rush nearly had their own incinnati when tickets for their ebruary 17 show went on sale at the assive Cobo Hall in Detroit on aturday, January 12.

There were between 1,000 and 1,500 ids waiting in line to buy tickets when e box office was opened at 8.30 a.m. – n hour and a half earlier than the lanned time. The box office manager ad opened early because of the crowd, me of whom – according to local olice – had been waiting all night in ear freezing temperatures. With eight olice on duty the crowds rushed the oors, smashed the glass in six of them nd tore another two literally off their inges.

Another dozen cops were called and estored order with the judicious use of nightsticks – the lengthier American version of the humble truncheon. To get people to move back they hit them on the legs with their clubs.

Through some sort of minor miracle no-one was seriously injured although several reported being trampled to the ground. Eventually all 20,029 tickets for the gig were sold out.

At about the same time Rush had made it clear in the American press that they were concerned to a very great extent with the question of safety of their audiences at concerts.

Rush specified in their contracts that there would be no "festival seating" – which is an American promoters' euphemism for taking out the seats and squeezing as many people as possible into a gig without regard for safety.

Said Geddy Lee: "It's really ignorant. It's treating kids like cattle, which they're not. It's something we've fought for a long time but nobody listens to you. They need a horrible tragedy like this (The Who Cincinnati incident) before they'll go 'Oh yeah, maybe you're right'.

"We've complained on a lot of our past shows. Can't we please have reserved seating all the time, but unfortunately no-one really paid attention until this incident happened."

Lee concluded "You never hear of riots in reserved seating. That's really what it boils down to."

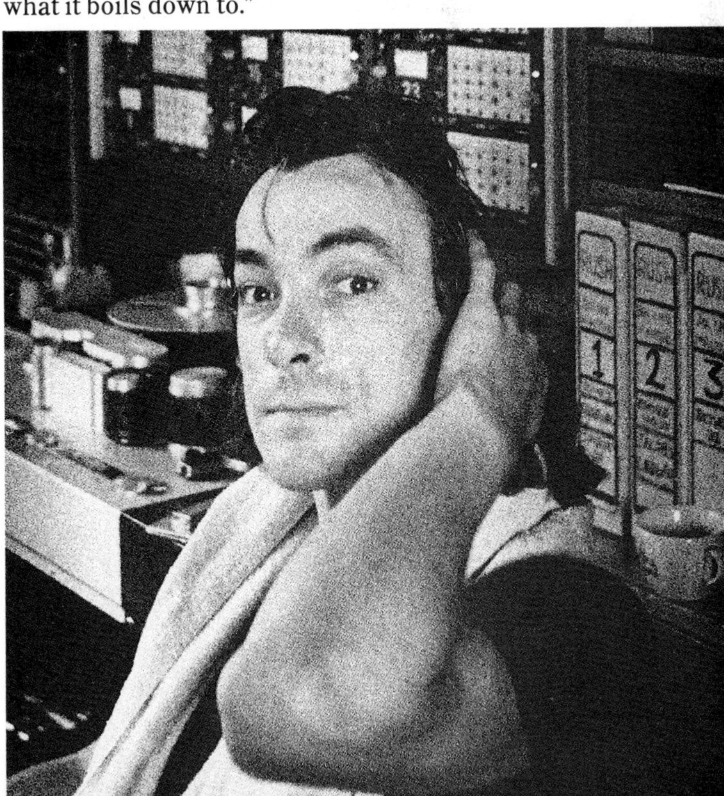

Neil Peart echoed Geddy's feelings. "I'm very happy we have a clause in our contract that allows for no festival seating. I tried to go for it during the last tour because over the past few years I have been watching people go through so much suffering at the front of the stage – people being pulled out of the audience by their feet and people just being pushed back and forth. It's terrib to watch."

Despite their reserved seating only contract rider; Rush still managed to pu in some incredibly vast crowds on thei American tour – the biggest they'd eve attracted and proof positive that they were a massive band.

Just take a look at some of the

igures. Down in Wichita they pulled in ,300 kids at the Kansas Coliseum. In os Angeles at the Inglewood Forum hey attracted more than 10,000 who aid a total of 102,000 dollars to see the and. On their West Coast section of heir tour Rush pulled in more than 1,000 fans.

The Cleveland Coliseum saw them before an 18,000 strong audience, Edmonton had 15,000, Fort Worth in Texas 13,000 and so on.

They played four nights in Chicago, four in New York, two in Seattle – all this went on from January through until May. Perhaps the most startling area of all was St Louis. They played three nights in the town, the first time any rock band

had played a major venue there three times in a row, and all told 30,000 local inhabitants saw their two hour plus show.

In one week alone – February 13 to 19 – the band generated more than half a million dollars worth of ticket sales – 584,095 to be exact – with those remarkable series of shows in St Louis and Detroit making more than 200,000 and 250,000 dollars respectively.

The pattern was repeated all across the country. But if the figures seem spectacular – which they are, to be honest – what's even more surprising is that later Alex Lifeson was to say that the 'Permanent Waves' tour was the first one from which Rush actually showed a profit.

That was undoubtedly due to the sheer scale of the Rush touring operation. They travelled around America with some 600,000 dollars worth of stage gear, sound equipment and that light show, plus a road crew in the region of two dozen - all of which was transported in four big trucks, a couple of buses and a magnificently appointed camper boasting just about anything the 1980s traveller could desire.

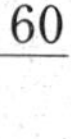

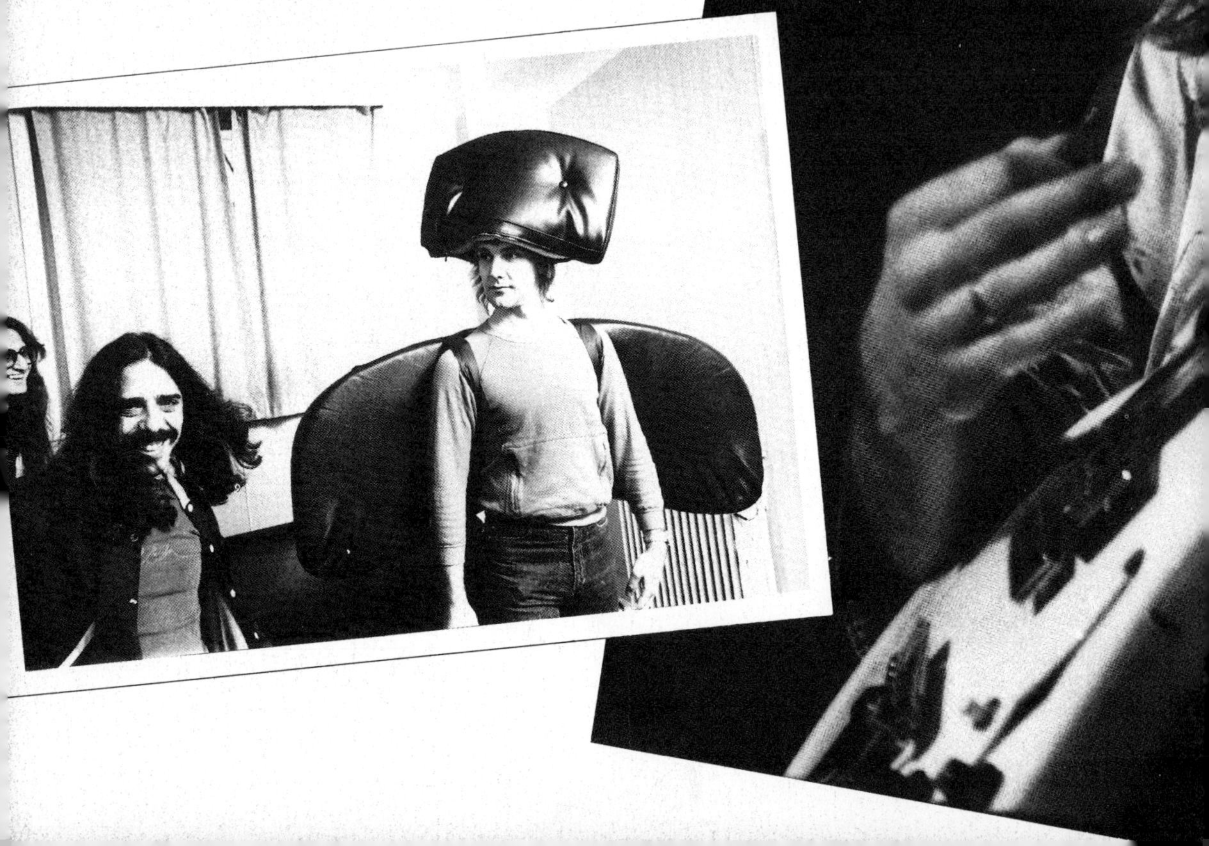

If the sheer statistics of the 'Permanent Waves' tour are impressive the turn-about in the attitude of the critics on the other side of the Atlantic was equally impressive. The band were finally recognized in most quarters as one of the most impressive outfits stage-wise on the road. In addition, Neil Peart's lyrics and the sheer, outstanding musicianship of all three members were getting the attention and the praise they had deserved for so long.

The Cleveland show was rated as one of the finest performances ever seen in the town. "Rush" said the reviewer "lives up to, and also sets, standards that all touring bands of the Eighties must follow."

In Wichita the local critic raved over their "phenomenal musicianship" while in Calgary the reviewer felt that Rush had showed a capacity crowd that "heavy metal was far from dead." As a final example, down in St Louis it was said that Rush had progressed "into one of the foremost musical forces and performing ensembles in the world." The writer added that the band had entered "an élite circle at the pinnacle of international rock."

Of course it wasn't all rave reviews. The Kansas City man felt that Rush were predictable, too loud and too reliant on visual and musical spectacle. The reporter added that the band had "brought down the house, nevertheless."

Up in New York State the *Rochester Democrat and Chronicle* popular arts editor, Jack Garner, reserved a special mention for Geddy. Having trashed the band generally he moved on to specifics. "The hardest thing to take is vocalist-bassist Geddy Lee whose voice MUST be an acquired taste. He sounds like Led Zeppelin's Robert Plant would sound if someone jumped off the other end of a seesaw."

It's probably fair to say that Rush themselves didn't much care about the reviews – good or bad. They'd been vindicated by the public and had no real need to worry about the professional pundits. Also, from a purely fiscal point of view, according to manager Ray Danniels, the band had started the tour around 300,000 dollars in debt and after it, for the first time in their careers they were completely in profit.

Danniels pointed out to a reporter in Toronto that the band could have made a lot more money, a lot earlier in their careers but it was their insistence on doing things their own way that had prevented them from doing so.

He said that the band insisted on playing smaller, less profitable gigs in areas which had been loyal to them in the past because they preferred to return that loyalty – at some financial cost to themselves – than go for the big bucks instantly. Given that – which to me, as a close observer of the band, seems fair and accurate – the mind reels back from the astronomical amount of money they could have made on that historic 'Permanent Waves' jaunt.

After the Los Angeles Forum show on that tour Rush were dragged back to a reception for the music biz where a reporter recorded them as holding themselves aloof from the others present. Neil was said to be continually looking for the exit, Geddy zipped into a remote corner and Alex popped himself into an alcove where people could "see him but not touch him."

Why? Because they hate events like this. Geddy was quoted as saying, at this particular event "Who are these people? I don't care if this is L.A. These people in radio, in the record industry, they never supported us getting here. The kids did. We were pressured into being here and smiling. We shouldn't be here."

I've seen them do much the same thing on several occasions in Britain – willing to take to people who had stuck with them throughout the leaner times: in fact, not so much willing as positively eager. But then, maybe an hour into the reception you turn round to see where they are and they've gone.

It's just that they're keen to avoid being wrapped up in the music business and if they've got time to spare after a gig they'd sooner spend it talking to kids and signing autographs than sit around with record company salesmen who are busily gulping down record company wine and scoffing record company food.

Says Neil: "We're finding it easier to say no. This can be a pretty sleazy business and I can understand people getting wrapped up in it all. But we've learned what we should do."

Perhaps Ray Danniels summed their attitude up best when he said "They may not go to cocktail parties and like it but they'll do the longest set in the business for the people who've paid for it."

The fans were repaying Rush in kind on the record sales front by making

'Permanent Waves' go gold in the States, platinum in Canada and silver in Britain – all within two months of the album's release.

Furthermore, in April 1980, *Sounds* and *Melody Maker* published the results of their annual readers polls. Rush and each individual member of the band were placed in the top ten of each applicable category in both polls – a magnificent achievement when the music papers were telling us that Johnny Rotten's new band Public Image Limited was the only group worth listening to.

However, among the music press there were certain specialist heavy metal writers who enthused mightily about 'Permanent Waves'. Malcolm Dome in *Record Mirror* said that while the album didn't quite reach "the classic heights of 'Hemispheres' nonetheless Lee, Lifeson and Peart have come up with half a dozen persuasive reasons for breaking out the champagne and celebrating the new decade".

Dome also recommended the album as an answer to punters who thought intelligent heavy metal was the figment

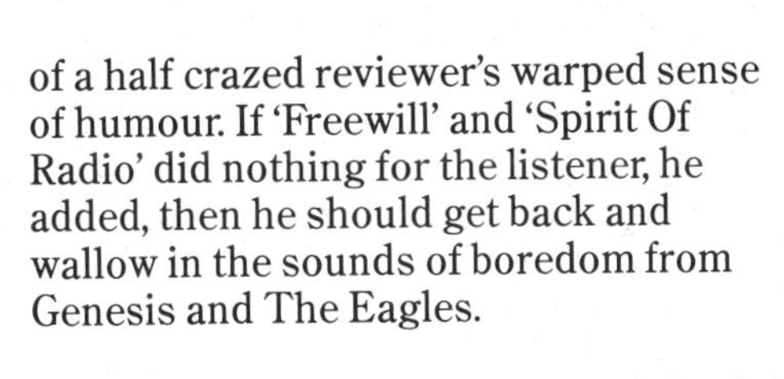

of a half crazed reviewer's warped sense of humour. If 'Freewill' and 'Spirit Of Radio' did nothing for the listener, he added, then he should get back and wallow in the sounds of boredom from Genesis and The Eagles.

John Gill in *Sounds* suggested that it was the Rush album to end all Rush albums. The album, he said, "finds Rush healthier than ever, fresher than ever and with a keen eye on the (ir) future. Gone are the days of the side-long epics and science fantasy myths, their place taken by Rush music 80's style, expert, awesome, energetic and aware."

Gill went on to suggest that 'Permanent Waves' could become Neil Peart's definitive statement – "as it's the most philosophical Rush album to date", and without the assistance of allegories straight off the shelves of 'Dark They Were And Golden Eyed' – the last being a store in London that specialised in science fiction books, magazines etc, much of which was on the 'sword and sorcery' side.

Melody Maker's Steve Gett zeroed in on the shorter length of the tracks, suggesting that if Rush had continued with their "mammoth tales of black holes in space" they might well have reached a stalemate.

Gett reckoned that 'Hemispheres' had been the closing stage of that particular phase of the band's career and that 'Permanent Waves' marked the beginning of a new one. However, Gett also entered a caveat concerning Neil's new lyrical subject matter, expressing pleasure that they weren't so contrived as in the past and that Neil was no longer delivering his messages in the guise of a Tolkien fantasy.

"But", warned Gett, "what he's writing now seems to imply social comment and one wonders whether Rush fans understand or care about what he's trying to say. I'm sure that listeners are more responsive to a Lifeson guitar solo than to erudite verse."

Naturally it was left to *NME* to come in with all guns blazing among the four major music papers in the UK. But, to be fair, reviewer Paul Du Noyer made a considerable effort to seek out what he considered the good parts of the album before slamming the bad bits.

Basically this boiled down to an acceptance of the music as being a good example of its genre but at the same time having an exceedingly wary and jaundiced view of Neil's lyrics and attitudes.

The album, said Du Noyer "can only serve to consolidate Rush's enormous popularity because it is undeniably superior high production heavy rock, powerful and glossy. Within the given limitations of the genre, this is inventive stuff, with a degree of intelligence and sensitivity that's not to be found around too many of their rivals."

But on the lyrics Du Noyer felt they were "hardly the substance of Art, however defined – more like the first faltering efforts of an averagely bright 13 year old who's deeply into Rod McKuen."

And, as far as the lyrics went to any kind of social or philosophical comment, Du Noyer was even less sure. He described the band's "proudly reactionary stance" as muddled and shallow – "an ill-argued dog's dinner of Plato, Milton Friedman and Patience Strong." Even if you don't like what Du Noyer was saying about Rush you've still got to admire his turn of phrase.

In the States the reviews were equally mixed with John Swenson, writing in *Creem,* definitely coming good on the side of those who hated it.

"Criticizing them" he wrote, referring to their past efforts "would have been like going fishing without water. But this grim Canadian trio has done something so remarkable I can no longer hold my tongue – after seven tries, Rush has finally made a good album."

Mind you, Swenson's idea of good probably wouldn't tally with most peoples ideas. In the context of 'Waves' he rates as good something which wouldn't make you forget The Rolling Stones but would make you glad that Emerson, Lake and Palmer had hung up their flying synthesisers.

"This", he said "is art rock in all its pretentious, desperately self-justifying glory – and lead singer Geddy Lee still sounds like an eunuch Jerry Vale at 78 rpm."

His final coup de grâce – in a review consisting of nothing but coups de grâce – was: "the band now clocks in a little ahead of Uriah Heep on the art rockometer, a substantial advance."

Rolling Stone's David Fricke was far more on the ball and to the point. He wrote: "It's easy to criticize what you can't understand which at least partly explains why Canadian power trio Rush have suffered so much at the hands of rock journalists since the band's début album in 1974." Fricke dished out praise all round and concluded with one of the most perceptive remarks ever committed to print by a rock journalist on the subject of Rush.

"Rush's problem has rarely been

competence. They simply don't play fashionable music. If they couldn't cut it on their own terms it would be different but this band is among the very best in its genre.

"And, if the Top Five status of 'Permanent Waves' is any example it's a genre wherein critics don't count at all."

And that's exactly the point the band were trying to make with the album and its title. Neil Peart said 'Permanent Waves' was intended as a dig at the British music press which, he reasoned, by virtue of being weekly was desperate for new people to write about every week. As a result the press was either killing off somebody or raising up someone else as the "unheralded new God."

Oddly enough at the same time Peart pointed out he didn't have it in for the New Wave which was an area which intrigued him. More than once he'd gone into print saying that Johnny Rotten had been a performer of enormous charisma and power with The Sex Pistols.

Said Geddy Lee, on the same subject as the album's title "As far as I can see, new wave, old wave, yellow wave – it's all the same. The water doesn't come and go. The waves do."

To sum up, the band's attitude to the press is perhaps given away on a part of the album cover which shows a newspaper blowing in the wind. The banner front page headline is a classic in the history of American newspapers. It refers to the result of the 1948 Presidential election – and the newspaper got the result wrong.

Still, if Rush didn't much like the British music press and the attitudes of most of its members they couldn't deny that they got plenty of coverage when their next British tour was announced.

The band were revealed as having a month long touring schedule in Britain for June, 1980. They opened at Southampton Gaumont (June 1 and 2), followed by five nights at London's Hammersmith Odeon (June 4 to 8), Glasgow Apollo (10 and 11), Newcastle City Hall (12 and 13), Leeds Queens Hall (15), Chester Deeside Leisure Centre (16), Manchester Apollo (17 and 18), Birmingham Odeon (20), Leicester De Montfort Hall (21) and Brighton Centre (22).

By the time the tour was announced ticket demand had already been quite remarkable. Simply on speculative mail order bookings, or information via word of mouth, Hammersmith Odeon had sold out for the first two nights, both shows at Glasgow Apollo had already gone and Newcastle City Hall reported that by the time their dates had been announced they'd had enough postal bookings to fill the place anyway.

Meantime the band was finishing off their five month American tour and considering what they were going to do

for their next live album.

It's interesting that their original thought was that it was about time for another live one – having enjoyed a lot of success with 'All The World's A Stage' which had been released nearly four years previously.

It could also have been that the band were feeling a little tired both mentally and physically after the considerable effort they'd put into making 'Permanent Waves' and then embarking on the subsequent, hectic tour of North America.

However, as Neil Peart records, towards the end of that tour something changed their mind about the next album. "It had been our announced intention to record and release a second live album but an unlooked-for charge of ambition and enthusiasm caused a last minute resolution to throw caution out of the window and dive headlong into the making of a studio LP instead.

"The reasons for this are difficult to put to paper, being somewhat instinctive, but all of us had been feeling very positive and our Research and Development Dept (sound check jams) had been very spirited and interesting, so it was felt that the creative hiatus provided by a live album was not really necessary at present and it would be more timely and more satisfying to embark on the adventure of a new studio album".

By the time the band got to the UK,

espite having decided not to make a ve album they found that the rrangements they'd made to record heir five nights at Hammersmith Odeon nd the concerts at Glasgow, Aanchester and Newcastle couldn't eally be changed without major hassles.

So they went ahead and recorded hem anyway and the plan was that hese tapes could be added to ecordings from the 1981 North American tour – they plan ahead, these guys – and maybe a live album could be extracted from that – a live album which vould live up to the exacting standards Rush set themselves.

I went to see the band twice at Hammersmith Odeon – it would have been all five nights but I couldn't get the tickets – and on the first one I felt just a bit concerned hat they were perhaps going through he motions. By the time I went to the second I realised they were doing no such thing. Instead they were working harder at pacing their set and trying to ntegrate the new material with the cataclysmic older stuff. It turned out to be a good tour for Rush, all told – but that was something they had still ahead of them when I went backstage at the Odeon to talk to them.

Backstage seemed orderly but overpopulated. There was no particular madness going on – just an awful lot more people than usual. I'd requested an interview with Alex and I was hanging around outside the dressing rooms while the road crew ushered in fans, six at a time and as smartly lined up as a bunch of Coldstream Guards at the Trooping of the Colour. The autographs were signed, the lucky six were wheeled out, expertly and efficiently and the next half dozen were ushered into the presence with equal precision. You had to admire the way it was done really – no pushing, no crushing and everyone got served.

It did mean hanging about for ages and when it finally came to talking time I found myself face to face with Neil. Of course I thought the interviews are done in strict rotation and I got Neil again. No matter – they're all good talkers.

We found a deserted dressing room and within a few minutes of small talk it was Peart who raised the hoary old topic of the *NME* interview with Miles and the whole crypto-fascist smear. I was surprised really because all of that was very much history.

"I look back on that and I still can't believe it" he said, shaking his head. "We were just having a good conversation discussing our political views and I was surprised at the way it came out in the paper. I guess it doesn't really bother me anymore and I guess I'm kind of tired talking about it. I mean I don't know what to say about it – you say what you like about the whole thing, you know enough about the band to get it right."

He perked up considerably when we talked about the band's ever increasing success rate all over the world, and particularly in the States where, I'd heard, radio stations were playing their stuff in significant quantities for the first time ever.

"We're seeing the results of all the hard work we've put in over the years" said Neil. "We've worked so hard at establishing ourselves in Britain, for example, that when we come over here now we expect to have a good tour. I don't want this to sound conceited in any way but we expect sell-out concerts and we expect good responses from the audience.

"We put in the work and now we're seeing the results. Of course if we did a bad show I wouldn't expect a good response, but I'd be really surprised if we did a bad show these days.

"In America I think a lot of the disc jockeys are being forced to play our songs now because the kids are phoning them up and demanding that they play them. For me that's ideal. I don't want a jock playing our material because the record company promotion man is his best friend, or his brother-in-law. I either want them to play it because they're into it, or better still, play it because the kids want to hear it.

"It's pleasant enough getting response from radio stations and from the American press now but I can't say that we're all too excited about it. It's okay but we're not about to start celebrating because some jock has finally discovered who we are – they all had plenty of chances over the last eight years, when we really needed them. Now, it's nice to have them but I can't say that we really need them, now when we have

audiences like the one we had here at Hammersmith and like so many of the crowds we're getting in America now.

"You know, it's tremendously satisfying to do well in Britain. It's not the most important market in the world in terms of record sales but we all have a special relationship with this country. I've lived here for a while, we've recorded several albums here and enjoyed doing them tremendously and we've also experienced a lot of loyalty from the fans. You really can't have a better relationship than that."

Neil was still keeping his options open concerning whether the next Rush album would be live or studio.

"We're recording much of this tour" he said "and if it works well we probably will do a live album. We've recorded shows before – apart from the 'All The World's A Stage' recordings – but somehow it really never went right.

"Speaking personally, whenever I got on stage I found myself being terribly conscious of the show being recorded and, as a result made some mistakes.

"But then I found that my mind was magnifying those mistakes to the point where none of the concerts seemed satisfactory. But now a live album seems a logical step and I think we're at an emotional and mental stage in our careers where we can do one with confidence and know that the end result will turn out to be good enough to please."

After their last show at Hammersmith the band were invited to a reception in their honour given by Phonogram, their UK record company, at the enormously swish Café Royal in Regent Street.

I popped down there as well and probably spent more time at the party than the band. They listened patiently to speeches, collected various silver discs, said a few polite words in return and then commandeered a couple of tables for themselves, their crew and their closest friends and basically insulated themselves from the rest of the room.

Having completed the British tour to a tumultuous response the band went back to Canada for a swift break and then trundled back into the studios to

kick ideas around for the next album.

By now they had definitely decided that a live album was not on the cards and were considering material for a studio one which they now keenly wanted to do.

At the end of July they were in Toronto's Phase One studios with Max Webster recording a song called 'Battlescar' for The Webster's next album. Peart described the sound the two bands made at full tilt as a "Wagnerian tumult". However, while they were in the studios, Pye Dubois, The Webster band's lyricist, presented Rush with a song of his. This eventually turned into a track called 'Tom Sawyer', one of the stand out cuts on the band's forthcoming album 'Moving Pictures'.

Following the pattern of work they'd established on 'Permanent Waves' the band went off to a quiet place, Stony Lake in Ontario, to rough out their musical and lyrical ideas for the new album. 'The Camera Eye' was the first to be composed, followed by 'Tom Sawyer', 'Red Barchetta', 'YYZ' and 'Limelight'.

'YYZ', incidentally, which I thought was something to do with chromosomes and genetics when I first heard it, turned out to be inspired by something far more mundane. It is, in fact, the international identity code for Toronto Airport. "The intro" says Neil "is taken from the Morse code which is sent out by the beacon there. It's always a happy day when YYZ appears on our luggage tags".

By the end of August the band was back in Toronto's Phase One studios with co-producer Terry Brown (alias Broon) where they put together demos of the five songs already mentioned and also a version of 'Witch Hunt' which turned out to win the Rush Award for the most re-written song in their repertoire.

"Our intention" he said, explaining

vhy they persisted with it, "had always)een to use it as the production number)f the album, in the tradition of such)ieces as 'Different Strings', 'Madrigal' ınd 'Tears'. This frees us from our usual)ractice of writing as we would play live, naintaining the discipline of a three)iece band."

The band brought in keyboard)layer Hugh Symes and what they called a "Vigilante Choir" in the show. Peart ıappily agrees that this particular track vas, and was always intended to be, "a small dose of studio indulgence."

The band took a break from recording in October and played a short tour, mainly of the East Coast of the United States. During that time they rehearsed the five finished songs as often as possible and introduced 'Tom Sawyer' and 'Limelight' into the set.

From October to December the band worked on finishing the album. They had to work hard at getting the finished versions of 'YYZ', 'Tom Sawyer' and 'Limelight' but, to their surprise, 'Red Barchetta' turned out right on the first take.

The last song to be done was 'Vital Signs'. The band had deliberately left themselves short of one track before they went into the studios having achieved such good results, writing in the studio, with past works like 'Natural Science' and 'The Twilight Zone'. Neil describes the inspiration for the song as "my response to the terminology of 'Technospeak', the language of electronics and computers, which often seems to parallel the human machine in the functions and interrelationships they employ."

Obviously the machines felt that Neil was getting close to finding something out about them because they rebelled at the mixing stage of 'Moving Pictures'. The digital mastering machine, the mixdown computer and one of the multi-track machines packed in one after the other driving the band and Terry Brown mildly insane and setting back the recording schedule by two weeks. Peart records he was glad to get it over with, "as with anything that drags on too long", but he expressed himself more than pleased with the outcome.

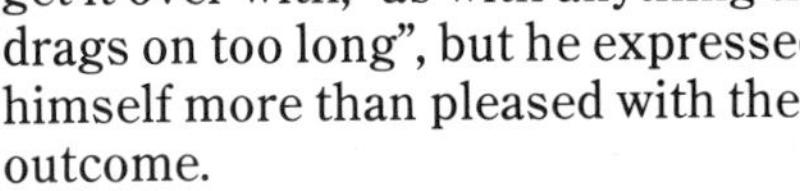

It's chastening to think, and a fascinating illustration of the standards of modern music, that a total of around six months work ended up producing just 40 minutes of recorded music.

With a brief break for Christmas and the start of 1981 the band embarked on a massive tour of North America in February to coincide with the simultaneous worldwide release of 'Moving Pictures'. Without going into too much detail, Rush's tour of America was their biggest yet and, for them, it was probably topped by appearing at New York's massive and prestigious Madison Square Garden – where only the very biggest bands have ever appeared.

By the end of the tour they were rated as one of the Top Four concert attractions in North America and were generally acknowledged as the top working heavy metal band.

They played their last date of that tour in July and then awarded themselves the luxury of an extended break. They weren't back on the road until October when they played a massive tour of the UK, not so much in number of gigs but the sheer size of venues – playing multiple dates in the biggest arenas Britain could offer, like Stafford Bingley Hall and Wembley Arena.

To coincide with that they finally got out their live album, 'Exit... Stage Left'. The band had done what they promised

which was to take recordings from the last British tour and combine them with tapes from the North American tour.

Talking to Alex at Bingley Hall – I finally picked the right time on the interviewing rota! – he told me that the live one was very much a Terry Brown project.

"It was really his baby . . . we would just kind of drop in now and again, make a few suggestions and wander out again.

"Of course there was a lot of thought put into the selection of tracks. There were some things we didn't really want to hear again and there were others that had already been included on 'All The World's A Stage'. But finally I think we came up with something pretty satisfying". That judgement was heartily endorsed by the British public who ordered 40,000 copies of the album before it was released.

Talking to Alex and looking at the band on the tour I got the impression that I was dealing with a group of people who had finally achieved everything they had wanted when they first started out in a small Ontario township all those years ago.

America, Britain, Japan, most of Europe – all the major markets in the world had fallen to them and they were rated among the best and most successful bands in the world by legions of fans.

They had achieved sufficient confidence in themselves to entrust the completion of their live album to Terry Brown. Admittedly he's just about the fourth member of the band but time was when I doubt if they'd have even allowed their immediate family to take a hand in their professional careers.

They were looking forward to taking more time off, cutting down their touring schedule from ten months a year to maybe a more manageable six.

And then there were the solo projects. Said Alex: "I have a 16 track studio being completed downstairs in my house at the moment and when it's ready I think I might have a try at some solo material".

Geddy and Neil are considering individual projects too. Neil is very interested in writing at the moment – not song writing but doing things for magazines, short stories and so on. And Geddy will probably find himself doing production for other bands since he's very interested in that field.

"As for the band, at the beginning of '82 I guess we'll take ourselves somewhere up to the frozen north of Canada and settle down to writing. I don't think we'll have more than the usual trouble in getting enough material."

Since then the band, for Rush, have been relatively quiet.

The first half of '82 saw them writing, touring in America, checking out new talent to sign to their own Anthem label, continuing on their solo projects and considering how best to hit those parts of Europe which have hitherto not fallen quite as conclusively as the rest under the Rush sway.

As usual there have been rumours in the music press about them playing major festivals here, about massive tours, about upcoming albums.

But Rush, as ever, take their time. They've worked too hard and too long to hurry things now. Their standards are higher than ever, their approach as honest as ever, their concern for fans as high as ever.

For me they're one of the best bands ever to come along in rock and roll. They'll probably continue for years yet, as inventive as ever, entering Phase Four Five and Six of their careers with equal style and consideration as the first three. As far as I'm concerned they can carry on forever. Hope you agree.